THE **KITCHEN** BOOK
OF 21 POSTCARDS

Salmo trutti

SAN FRANCISCO • CALIFORNIA

Salmo trutti

P.O. BOX 280070
SAN FRANCISCO • CALIFORNIA 94128-0070

ISBN: 1-56313-874-3
TITLE #: ST874

Salmo trutti publishes a large line of photographic books and postcard books.
Please write for more information.

Printed in Korea

THE KITCHEN BOOK OF 21 POSTCARDS

PUBLISHED BY *Salmo trutti* • SAN FRANCISCO, CALIFORNIA

THE KITCHEN BOOK OF 21 POSTCARDS

PUBLISHED BY *Salmo trutti* • SAN FRANCISCO, CALIFORNIA

THE KITCHEN BOOK OF 21 POSTCARDS

PUBLISHED BY *Salmo trutti* • SAN FRANCISCO, CALIFORNIA

THE KITCHEN BOOK OF 21 POSTCARDS

PUBLISHED BY *Salmo trutti* • SAN FRANCISCO, CALIFORNIA

THE KITCHEN BOOK OF 21 POSTCARDS

PUBLISHED BY *Salmo trutti* • SAN FRANCISCO, CALIFORNIA

THE KITCHEN BOOK OF 21 POSTCARDS

PUBLISHED BY *Salmo trutti* • SAN FRANCISCO, CALIFORNIA

THE KITCHEN BOOK OF 21 POSTCARDS

PUBLISHED BY *Salmo trutti* • SAN FRANCISCO, CALIFORNIA

THE KITCHEN BOOK OF 21 POSTCARDS

PUBLISHED BY *Salmo trutti* • SAN FRANCISCO, CALIFORNIA

THE KITCHEN BOOK OF 21 POSTCARDS

PUBLISHED BY *Salmo trutti* • SAN FRANCISCO, CALIFORNIA

THE KITCHEN BOOK OF 21 POSTCARDS

PUBLISHED BY *Salmo trutti* • SAN FRANCISCO, CALIFORNIA

THE KITCHEN BOOK OF 21 POSTCARDS

PUBLISHED BY *Salmo trutti* • SAN FRANCISCO, CALIFORNIA

THE KITCHEN BOOK OF 21 POSTCARDS

PUBLISHED BY *Salmo trutti* • SAN FRANCISCO, CALIFORNIA

THE KITCHEN BOOK OF 21 POSTCARDS

PUBLISHED BY *Salmo trutti* • SAN FRANCISCO, CALIFORNIA

THE KITCHEN BOOK OF 21 POSTCARDS

PUBLISHED BY *Salmo trutti* • SAN FRANCISCO, CALIFORNIA

THE KITCHEN BOOK OF 21 POSTCARDS

PUBLISHED BY *Salmo trutti* • SAN FRANCISCO, CALIFORNIA

THE KITCHEN BOOK OF 21 POSTCARDS

PUBLISHED BY *Salmo trutti* • SAN FRANCISCO, CALIFORNIA

THE KITCHEN BOOK OF 21 POSTCARDS

PUBLISHED BY *Salmo trutti* • SAN FRANCISCO, CALIFORNIA

THE KITCHEN BOOK OF 21 POSTCARDS

PUBLISHED BY *Salmo trutti* • SAN FRANCISCO, CALIFORNIA

THE KITCHEN BOOK OF 21 POSTCARDS

PUBLISHED BY *Salmo trutti* • SAN FRANCISCO, CALIFORNIA

THE KITCHEN BOOK OF 21 POSTCARDS

PUBLISHED BY *Salmo trutti* • SAN FRANCISCO, CALIFORNIA